In Advent

Books by A. Poulin, Jr.

The American Folk Scene: Dimensions of the Folksong Revival (Editor, with David A. DeTurk), 1967

Contemporary American Poetry (Editor), 1971

Making in All Its Forms: Contemporary American Poetics and Criticism (Editor), 1972

In Advent: Poems, 1972

IN ADVENT
Poems

A. Poulin, Jr.

E. P. DUTTON & CO., INC. | NEW YORK | 1972

First Edition

Copyright © 1963, 1965, 1967, 1968, 1969, 1970, 1971, 1972
by A. Poulin, Jr.

All rights reserved. Printed in the U.S.A.

No part of this publication may be reproduced or transmitted in any form
or by any means, electronic or mechanical, including photocopy, recording
or any information storage and retrieval system now known or to be in-
vented, without permission in writing from the publisher, except by a
reviewer who wishes to quote brief passages in connection with a review
written for inclusion in a magazine, newspaper or broadcast.

Published simultaneously in Canada by
Clarke, Irwin & Company Limited, Toronto and Vancouver

SBN: 0-525-13207-4

Library of Congress Catalog Card Number: 70-179846

To the editors of the following publications in which these poems first appeared, the author makes grateful acknowledgement:

THE ATLANTIC MONTHLY: "The Dream"; BITTERROOT: "Famine: 1966"; CHICAGO REVIEW: "Midwest Triptych" and "Eggs"; CHOICE: "To My Students," "Sunday Morning," "Assistant Professor Plots Revenge," "Against Spring," and Part II of "Angelic Orders," originally entitled "Clocks Are Angels, Too"; COLLEGE ENGLISH: "Landscape," "If We Pause," "Biddeford Pool," "Snowstorm: Biddeford Pool," and "Sons of Witches"; COMMONWEAL: "To E P (K)"; CONCERNING POETRY: "I Woke Up. Revenge" and "Sailing from Byzantium"; CRAZY HORSE: "Paratrooper"; DECEMBER: "Script Prospectus"; ESQUIRE: "The Coming"; THE JOURNAL OF POPULAR CULTURE, Vol. V (Bowling Green (Ohio) State University Popular Press): "Buddha and the Pirates" and "Death and Transfiguration"; THE KENYON REVIEW: Part I of "Angelic Orders"; NEW AMERICAN REVIEW #5: "The Front Parlor"; NEW AMERICAN REVIEW #8: "The First Day"; NEW LETTERS: THE UNIVERSITY REVIEW: "Fear Survey Schedule"; THE NORTH AMERICAN REVIEW: "Toward Exorcism," "On His Unborn Child," and Parts 1, 2, 4 and 5 of "In Advent"; POETRY NORTHWEST: "Fish" and "In the Beginning"; SHENANDOAH: The Washington and Lee University Review: "Flute Making" and "Bombardier"; SOU'WESTER: "Memorial," "The Gleaner," and "Famine: 1970."

"Easter Sunday" originally appeared in a broadside series published by The Slo Loris Press.

"Totem" originally appeared in a broadside series published by The Valley Press.

The inscription for "Angelic Orders" is from *The Duino Elegies* by Rainer Maria Rilke translated by David Young which originally appeared in *Field: Contemporary Poetry and Poetics* and is reprinted by permission of the translator and the journal's editor, David Young.

The inscription by Robert Bly for "The Dream" is from "Looking into a Face" in *The Light Around the Body* © 1967 by Robert Bly and is reprinted by permission of Harper & Row, Publishers.

The inscription by James Dickey for "The Dream" is from "Springer Mountain" in *Helmets* © 1962 by James Dickey and is reprinted by permission of Wesleyan University Press.

The inscription for "The First Day" is from *The First Nine Months of Life* © 1962 by Geraldine Lux Flanagan and is reprinted by permission of Simon and Schuster, Inc.

The inscription for the "The Gleaner" is from "maggie and milly and molly and may" in *95 Poems* © 1958 by e. e. cummings and is reprinted by permission of Harcourt Brace Jovanovich, Inc.

Personal Acknowledgments

Hugh L. Hennedy, my first teacher
Ned Arnold, Marvin Bell, John Logan and George Starbuck
and Basilike: love, this one especially is yours too.

In memory of my father
and
for my mother

Contents

Angelic Orders

In Advent

Toward Exorcism

The Front Parlor

For Jo and Ken

Whenever someone in our family
died, the wake was in our house,
downstairs, in the front parlor.

It was a spare room, really, and,
except for a few extra folding chairs,
empty and unheated. The shades were

always drawn, the best lace curtains
hung. And in that constant cool
twilight, the wallpaper damp

as banks of carnations, when we
dared to go in, forbidden to,
we played like shadows beneath

the great cross, that enormous
suffering, dying or dead Christ,
the room's only constant ornament.

It never was a living room.

❋

I've slept above the dead before,
my bed in the same far corner
as their caskets. Assured their lips

were sewn, their arms clamped,
I've fallen asleep to the rhythm
of hummed rosaries. My grandfather

choosing to die on New Year's Day.
His wife, big boned and stubborn,
paralyzed for fifteen years,

bedridden five, decaying three,
gangrene growing on her back
like some warm carnivorous herb.

An uncle who never spoke a word
until the week he died, insane,
babbling the poison of his liver.

❋

I've slept above the dead enough.
Whole generations of a tribe. Still,
in the middle of the night, I hear

the prayers of the living and the dead,
a crescendo through the floorboards,
filling my room like an ancestral chorus:

*Que les âmes des défunts
reposent en paix par la miséri-
corde de Dieu.* They have burned

the seams of their eyes, chewed
the nylon thread threaded through
their lips. They have cast off

their clamps. They stand at my
bedside every night moaning my name
off endless strings of beads, burning.

She plants a growing kiss on my forehead.
With her green hand, moist as moss,
wide as my skull, and, forever free,

she strokes my back and thigh.

    ✦   ✦   ✦

To My Aunt

All through your life
    they lied to you. They said
        a baby sitter'd dropped you

and never told your
    mother. They never could
        admit that you were crippled,

born deformed, your shoulder
    jutting out into the blade
        of a stunted wing. Therefore,

they said, you could never
    lead a normal life, and,
        therefore, you never did.

Mutant of our crippled
    wills and hearts, you played
        tribal nurse and clown,

the fool of our cruelty and needs.
    I don't think you ever knew.
        Today we buried you.

No. You were even spared
    that simple fact: ice sealed
        the ground, a clenched and final

pack of lies. But you
    are dead, and, dead, leave
        me obsessed by that bump

and bright lie on your back.
    After they pronounced you
        dead, drained your blood

out of your veins and dressed
    you like a helpless child,
        was it impossible for them

to close that cage? Did
    your arms, furious, push back
        the leaded lid? Did they raise

you, then, turn you over,
    and with a hammer gently
        crack the cartilage of your wing?

Poor dead thing,
    we should have told you all
        along that you were only partly

human. Then, maybe,
    neither girl nor angel,
        that one thrust of yours

bandaged by your skin,
    with its invisible, burning
        mate, might have grown, grown

larger than your frame.
    Before we'd had a chance
        to break that wild wish

riding on your back,
    you could have winged
        yourself away from our lies.

Instead, what you were
    and always will be now
        always will be trapped

inside the mausoleum
    of our fabricated memory
        until they bury all of us.

But tonight, before
    the ground has thawed, before
        they stuff you in its mouth,

rigid as an owl
    at dawn, let me open up
        your cage; let me touch

both sides of your wound
    -ed back; let me heal
        you. Oh, with the moon

cracking on the snow
    and all your sisters
        chained to their dying

husbands, sleeping,
    let me show you now
        the truth about yourself.

Just once *believe*
    the light you feel
        trembling behind you.

Let that inhuman
    power carry you. *Do
        it. Try. Slowly now,*

*easy. Rise, yes.
    More. Oh, yes. Now
        hover. Soar. Fly! Fly!*

*   *   *

The Year of the Pueblo

To my sister, Anne

All day the dead are still.
Anchored in the hangar
in the hillside, their arms

clamped wings of wild
prehistoric birds
at the bottom of the sea,

they rock, gentle with the tides,
the tilting earth and winds,
invisible and benign.

It's at night, when nothing
living moves, when mirrors
open up like caskets

that they start. Whining,
trembling, the fuel of
their familiar fury burns,

and they sail, horizontal,
moving at inhuman speeds.
Their feet propel them.

The whole armada of our
clan invades my lawn
churning like the sea,

the few fathoms of air
I claim as mine. Huge
and deadly destroyers,

they violate my skull's
sovereignty I've fought for
for years. Anne, tonight

they've come to fight and win.
I feel the infrared blinking
of their eyes in mine. And,

ready to launch the torpedoes
of their hearts, the humming
of their spinning ribs tracks

my heart beat, beat by beat.

*   *   *

To My Brother

For Normand and Betty

You'd think there was no end to this
tribe. They set out and multiplied
as if survival of their species

depended on the acid of their sperm.
Now, in the middle of the night,
they call us to come bury their dead.

So we make that black pilgrimage
back to Lisbon to slide one more
familiar corpse into the holy hillside.

We've buried twelve of them, a dozen
deaths survived, with still a dozen more
or so to live through. The horror

of their deaths and lives lives on
and haunts us: Mandia bent and stunted
by that monster riding her shoulder,

lied into believing she was partly angel;
Blackie drunk before his couple suns
rose every morning of his life, except

the last; and Larry loving various wives,
not one of them his own, his children
strangers to him even when he died;

one Emile lingering for months in
hospital beds infested with leukemia's
piranha, another dropping on the corner

during lunch-hour, gaping blindly back
at the mill hands watching our father
take him in his arms and whisper the act

of contrition to his stone-deaf head.
Time and time again I resurrect them.
They gather in my head, eat, drink and

sing, celebrating their own wakes,
prolonging our interminable deaths.
But each time I return from burying one

of them, all the way back home from
Lisbon I can feel unknown and un-
remembered parts of me vanish in the dark

and exhausted silence behind me.
They die, Normand. They die.
And, dying, they kill our only history.

❋   ❋   ❋

The Survivor

My body doesn't want to breathe.

Birds are nesting in my lungs.
You know what birds can do
when they school in your exhaust.
But living, after all's, hard
work —all those cubic feet
of oxygen to pump, my throat
a whining iron lung. And on
winter afternoons the white lotus
of carbon monoxide blooms, while
in the same monotonous gallons
of old blood, corpuscles coagulate
into pearls and stall in arteries.

Still, I lecture it: If you don't
breathe, you'll die. I think
my body wants to die. I do.

❄   ❄   ❄

Hunters

Fall. Fields and forests
tremble with the blasts
of shotguns. The orange
ghosts of hunters burn new
trails through the morning
mist. At noon, high above
the bay, Canadian geese
soar, precise, victorious.

The time has come.
I strip down to
my waist, and, stalking
hunters, roam the fields.

Inside my ribs, iridescent
as a cock pheasant,
my father's cancer flutters.

* * *

Medium

To Sylvia Plath

You've obsessed me long enough.
Sister, wife and mother,
your book's a box of furious bees,
a casket humming in my study.
Your cry inhabits me,
a piston in my chest.
Your words grapple in my throat
or fall, ashes in the pupils
of my eyes. Mad, posthumous
medium, for weeks you've been
my thesaurus and my cornea.

Sylvia, from your limbs and roots
you built your purest fire.
It killed you. But while dying,
another Salem witch or Jew,
you taught us what it is
to burn. The fire made you
precious. Purified, baby, sleep.

❖   ❖   ❖

Homecoming

For Hugh Hennedy

I come back to my friends.
They're glad to see me.
They throw parties in my honor
and offer me good jobs.
Their wives want to make love
to me, and I'm happy, until
one day we're stranded
by a blizzard, bound to one
another, a family of lost
orphans in a fairy tale.

In one afternoon we talk
for months before a dying
fire. I play the witch.
Then they start squinting.
Their eyes are failing me.
Their wives notice the small
wrinkles near my ears,
and they move off the couch,
their warmth still on my thighs.
Another hour, drink and log,
and I'm really out of focus.

Once upon a time I was pre-
cisely etched on the contact
lenses of their memory,
but I've strained the edges
of that stencil with a word
or a forgotten gesture.

The fire roars. The whiskey
burns. The witch will never
win. I can feel myself
cracking in their corneas,
melting in their throats
and burning at the stake.

❋   ❋   ❋

Buddha and the Pirates

1

Enshrined in a doorway,
your eyes blue as Ming
chips, you sit cross-legged,
fleshy, round and ringed,
a Buddha bulging
with miraculous paps.
Enameled angels wait
on you, bringing you huge
babies to be nursed, six
at a time, all orphans.
There are so many you can
never satisfy them all.
So, in a slow, deliberate
gesture of beneficence,
you recline on your side,
smile, and grow as many
breasts as your torso can
support, suffer babies
to be brought to you
until you start to tremble,
grace flowing out of you.

2

Our lawn is a green sea
we sail alone, second storey
explorers. Defenseless
in our pullman sloop,
we search for coves
and inlets, the peninsulas
of our marriage's continent.

We never heard them come.
We never even saw the skull
and crossbones of their black
flag glowing above their sails.

They swing on the masts
of trees, arms flashing
like sabers, and, soaring
on the red wings of sleeves,
their captain lands in our room.

Swashbuckler, he smiles
a flashing smile, assured
as Douglas Fairbanks. He says:
"You need me." Your hand
on your hip, you laugh at him
defiantly. Your eyes burn
green; your hair's flaming red.
You're as beautiful and brave
as Maureen O'Hara.

              He stokes
your hair. His fingers are
at home in that fire. I call
him scoundrel, but he hauls
you to himself like precious
spoil. His mates are laughing,
multicolored in the trees. Grey,
I'm not strong enough to fight
him off and watch the two of you
sail off toward the open sea.

3

Morning sails into our bedroom, the splintered
ghost of a Venetian ship.
You aren't here. I find
you in the sunlight
of the alcove. Once more,
across the ocean of my
deepest nightmare, you've
come back, our baby at your
breast. Love, my Buddha,
you are always here.

*   *   *

TO: E P (K)

Like dust on table corners
left by Martha's old black hand,
you linger, unseen,
on the edges of my brain.
But when the light is right,
slanting at oppressive angles,
and disturbs the silent shadows
in my room and skull,
I see you, and I'm embarrassed.
I make excuses to my friends:
"Forgetfulness is hard
to come by these days."
And with an unobtrusive
sweep of my own hand
I brush your name aside,
or cover up my memory
with some small book.

❋   ❋   ❋

Eggs

You were bigger than me.
Your front teeth were separated,
and you could whistle through them.
In the summer, when we drank
from the faucet near the barn,
you could squirt the water
through your teeth, one long
stream, clear as a whistle.
You were Uncle Larry's favorite.

You were stronger than me.
You could carry two baskets
full of eggs, one in each hand,
carry them downstairs even
in winter without slipping.
I slipped once, and the eggs
cackled on the ice like
a hundred melting suns.

You were older than me.
One day while Uncle Larry
slept under a tree, a messenger
from God, you took me, your captive
cowboy, to your hen-house tent
where the dust was piled as high
as sunlight, and like a savage man
of medicine, with a feather's blade
you opened up a wound in me

to rid my body of the arrow-
head. Then you taught me how
to leave a figure larger than life,
an angel for my camouflage.

*   *   *

The First Day

For Peter Fiore

*At least twenty million and often as many as five
hundred million sperm cells should be present in
a single ejaculation.*
                                        —*G. L. Flanagan*

Under the proper clinical conditions
I could have populated planets,
made Solomon look impotent
and the Seven Tribes of Judah sound
like the litter of a pampered bitch.

Patristic coverage would've been fantastic:
"On the first day, with his first ejaculation,
he begat five hundred million sons
and daughters. On the first day
with his third ejaculation he begat
three hundred million sons and daughters.
On the first day, with his fifth ejaculation,
he begat . . ." On and on, riding inspired
rhythms until the last ejecta left me
exhausted and expiring like some ancient
fish at the mouth of a high and spring-
fed river in the wildest wood.

High in the Maine woods instead,
on those hot days, while blue-
berries bled on my back, while
the screech of cicadas rose
to an inhuman pitch, while fish
suffocated in the pond, hounds

howling at the moon, lost, and
while the sun annihilated
galaxies spinning in my skull,

as I moaned   they came
dying on the desert
of my chest   they came
dying on my burning
rocks   dying
they   came
in the oven of my hand.

Oh   my   sons
     and   daughters
I   called   you
to   be   food   for
the   worms   of   this   earth.

   ✱   ✱   ✱

Toward Exorcism

To Rev. R.D., S.S.S.

I can hear you pacing
up and down between
our beds every night.

Your shoes are silent,
as if, every night, you,
like a mystic, suffer

levitation for our sakes
and souls, and, chaste,
your body is as light

as dust, as silent
as the dark you are.
Only your rosary clicks.

You finger your beads:
dried bones of foetus
answer your prayers.

In this third storey
hall hung with dead
Christs, three times

removed from both
the city and the world
below, we lie in rows,

sleepless as saints.
A bloodless bat,
you are our guardian

angel rustling nearby,
Gabriel at the door
of Eden, sword in hand,

driving us back in
until we have no choice
but to invent our sin.

＊   ＊   ＊

I Woke Up. Revenge

I woke up. Revenge was in my mouth.
I said my prayers. It tasted good,
familiar, old. I didn't feel afraid.

I have survived ten years of stale
nicotine and gin, a decade of most
kinds of sin. But I can't brush it
off my teeth or gargle it out of my throat.

And on my tongue revenge still sits,
a recalcitrant wedge of thinnest bread,
a stubborn, undissolving vatican.

❋   ❋   ❋

Fear Survey Schedule

Sons of Witches

The rat's angelic chatter in the attic
and the furnace moaning its white fire
are familiar winter choruses in this
New Hampshire house shedding a century
of paint. And when the wind has died,
and if we hold our breath, from
the forest's heart of ice we can hear
the soft sweet vowels of the witches,
singing as they burn.
                    Tonight the dark is
heavy on our lips, a yard of ground frozen
solid to its burning core. The white breath
of snow sprouts between the rocks; and chairs,
angel-headed tombstones glowing pale
as ice in moonlight, crouch. Under our
inherited handcarved headboard, waiting
for the slow loosening of our muscles'
rigor, we lie still as still warm corpses
waiting for another song, a warmth, a sleep.

* * *

Midwest Triptych

We've been below
the zero point
for days now, locked
in the massive
cold front above
Kansas. Mornings
are blunt ice.
We suck our words,
and, fired glass,
our passion cracks.
At noon the seas
at our sides
are bubbling hot
springs, oases.

This is my house.
I like it cold.
Tonight I sit
in the alcove,
do what I love
to do: listen
to the furnace
fail like heaven.
Radiators,
coiled and hollow,
hiss, a pack
of earnest priests.

In the mirrors
of my windows
leaded with ice,
I see three
treacherous
reflections
of myself.

●　　●　　●

Yes, George,

every night when my wife
and daughter are asleep
and I'm alone in this old house
lost in landscapes somewhere
between the points of stars,
every winter, every night
my furnace fails like heaven.

The water that will turn
to steam and turn to heat
and rise as grace runs out.
In unlighted corners, angles
opening to blank black space,
radiators, cold and white,
are silent as dead angels,
incarnate where they fell.

Every night, every winter,
I have to go down cellar,
turn the valve until the gauge
is full of water once again,
until the furnace starts
to rumble with its resurrection.
Then the house begins to move,
and through the winter night
that threatens us like Hell, by God,
the pure spirit of the fire roars,
blue, veins ring, and radiators,
a whole chorus of Dominions, sing
and dance wild alleluias warm as spring.

For George Starbuck

❅   ❅   ❅

Biddeford Pool

For Alan Mariani

> *Whoever you are, to you endless announcements!*
> —*Walt Whitman*

This fish-shaped village
of some ten or twenty
fishermen might be another
Paumanok for some other poet.

Standing in the marshes
near the ancient wharves
still smelling of the sea,
some queer split-tongued
bird of mysterious genesis,
he could stretch his neck
and sing large and rugged songs,
endless announcements of immor-
tality to the village fishermen.

But I've seen the way
these eight-fingered men look
at sea gulls and at cranes
when they return from mornings
spent on the horizon's edge.

Their eyes are blind with sunlight. Their tongues are split
with salt, their mouths white
with brine, as if they'd bitten
into death. Grunting and
lamenting, they haul in their nets
to repair them and their history.
And I know what they would do
to anyone who stood around
and sang and sang and sang.

*   *   *

Snowstorm: Biddeford Pool

Even through the heavy, blinding storm
the string of lights down the peninsula
shines like the borrowed spear of Patroklos
as it fished out Nestor's coward son
from his chariot's trembling pool of fear.

Up here, three stories higher than the bay
(where fishing boats are being tossed
like an armada sailing through some god's
revenge), I watch small flakes of snow pile up
on wharves, bloodless bodies of an endless war.

Come to fish themselves out of the pool
of blood, the well of memory pulsing in my chest,
the names of lost friends and lovers, a cache
of polished weapons, rattle in the dark.
Their faces shine and tremble with white wrath.
I am alone and cold. Afraid, I start to shiver.
I never did escape them and I never will.
Nothing, human or inhuman, can protect me.

Soon the lobsterman across the street will come
to the window in his underwear, looking like
some ancient warrior without armor. He'll
search the light breaking on the heaving,
stormed horizon of the sea, admit a vague,
inherited defeat, shrug, and grumble as he
tumbles back in bed beside his fish-eyed wife,
and roll his salty body toward her pool of oil.

❖   ❖   ❖

If We Pause

Today, again, he squats,
his transistor by his side.
He gathers acorns in a cotton
sack and selects his harvest
cautiously, polishing each
small fruit with a slow
awkward jerk of his elbow.

Most of us have seen him
in his father's store.
In pajamas, he sits behind
the counter in the corner.
Resting his large hands
on his groin, he strokes
the soiled flannel gently.

There beside the canned goods
by the cooler, near greeting
cards, among the newspapers
celebrating horror, he is
no less than fact:
an idiot boy; or, if
we pause, another mystery.

But today, as he works
beneath bronze oaks, crushing
leaves into a gold powder,
we have no taste for facts,
no time for mysteries
that will endure, outlast
the burning of this day.

We can't be blamed
for walking by him quickly.
We have good reason
to avoid his stare, to be
disturbed. He is an inter-
ruption, threat, a gargoyle
fallen like a sign.

❖   ❖   ❖

Memorial

1,000 COLLEGE STUDENTS' SUICIDES PREDICTED

    . . . psychological "pressure cooker"
    conditions on campus lead to many . . .
               —Iowa City Press Citizen

I sit in the Union
cafeteria (a memorial
for young men killed

in two world wars) grading
freshman papers. The table's
littered with the husks

of sandwich bags, the bones
of shredded thermo cups,
and ashes. The simmering

has started. Nearby a boy
trapped in concentration,
rakes his fingers through

his carrot hair, his shoulders
slowly softening to the late
October sun. By the windows

three girls collapse in chairs
and stretch their legs until
their skirts betray the white

pulp of their tender thighs.
And on the aluminum walls
moisture begins to bubble.

❊   ❊   ❊

To My Students

For John Logan

On these warm and humid summer nights
the echoes of your words swarm and buzz
around my brain. You are the mosquitoes
in the soft, strained light outside
my screened but opened window. Some of you,
the more ingenious perhaps, make your way
in. The others are no doubt victims
of a spider or the rain. Fascinated and
afraid, I watch you alighting gently
on my wrist: there among the scattered
hair as large as life, you probe for
blood beneath a tender spot of flesh.

How delicate your bodies and fragile
your frames fashioned somewhere in
the humid pulse of this warm night.
And how quickly, with almost invisible
wings, still damp, you circle toward
the light, and in birth blindness seek
the blood that some legend says is poison.
I pity you, although your small annoying
bodies are sometimes a relief from
the mounting monotony of memory.

And so, because I have some kind of cruel
love for you, a father's, I will let you
feed among the scattered hairs. But when I
can no longer bear your weight upon my wrist
or night upon my back, and because I always
thought (but never knew for certain) that
your death might be a long and painful
progress into day, I'll quickly crush you
with my fingertip before I flick the switch.

*   *   *

Assistant Professor Plots Revenge

That's what I'll do. I won't
sleep all night for two, three
days, a week. I'll drink too much
coffee till my teeth are brown
and dancing. I won't wash.

On the appointed day, I'll storm
into class looking like Isaiah
or the Baptist, my eyes cauldrons
full of boiling silver, my hair
flaming coils, my lips cracked
coals. And in that disguise
I'll address the multitudes
waiting for God's word, waiting
for the final solution to their
eternal crisis of identity.

I'll say: Listen, you multitudes,
waiting for The Word. Listen to me:
I've been in the desert forty
days and nights; I've slaked my
throat on dew gathering under rocks;
I've fed on the hind legs of locusts;
and I've had visions, visions I tell
you that seared my eyes. I saw branded
on the sky the flaming word of God.

I heard His voice like thunder saying:
"Tell this to the tide of multitudes."
And so, my multitudes, on this last
day of instruction, I'll tell you
what I saw. The word from heaven is:
YOU'RE A BUNCH OF FUCKIN IDIOTS!

●   ●   ●

Fear Survey Schedule

Sirs: In answer to your question-
naire, these are the things
and experiences that cause me
fear or other unpleasant feelings,
and the degree to which by every
one of them I am disturbed.

I am afraid of vacuum
cleaner noises not at all;
a fair amount of open wounds,
enclosed spaces and loud noises.
I am very much disturbed
by dentists, worms and reliquaries.
I am afraid of failure, falling,
and of being left alone, alot.

I am afraid of blood: a) human,
b) animal, very much; harmless
garden snakes, looking foolish,
of one person bullying another,
angry people, and of weapons.

Of journeys by: a) train, b) bus,
c) cars, I'm not too much
afraid —nor of strangers
and strange shapes, imaginary
creatures. And of sirens
I am not afraid at all.

Birds and bats and mice and cats
cause me unpleasant feelings,
as do commercials, jingles, prayers.

But I am very much afraid
of dead people, elevators,
of darkness and of lightning.
And, I'm afraid, I am afraid
of nude: b) women, a) men
in very high places, singing.

❋   ❋   ❋

The Last Day of the Year

In my green velour, gold crown
of hair, all day I've paced
the house, a domestic king
of sorts, delighting in my
explorations, my discoveries
and claiming them as mine.

This is my brown carpet,
my green fern, my bottle,
blue, the sea still tossing
in the glass. And my wife,
my beautiful young wife,
dark as an Egyptian queen,
hands winged with jewelry,
eyes as heavy as a sovereign's
makeup, lying on my bed
singing softly to herself
or to my newborn baby
at her other breast, my own
December child, still blind,
still mute and swaddled,
precious little mummy.

But tonight, while the ambulance
and plow spin their lights
of caution and disaster along
my street, around my living
room, all the objects I have

owned for years and years begin
to rise. They are the million
tiny mouths of snow, of earth,
the fierce red mouths of piranha
in my dreams. They are claiming
me and my claims for themselves.

❀   ❀   ❀

Landscape

We are gargantuan. The Old Man
of the Mountain and his rock-face
wife. Between us, under our eyes
steady as granite, the landscape
is deserted, a desert of wood grain
rippling like dunes to our breath.

On a plateau smooth as ceramic,
shadows of silos salt and pepper
the matchbox cottages, their
roofs bearing orange and purple
suns ceaselessly burning night
and day. Any day now the tinder
will ignite, raze this development
fabricated overnight, unpeopled.

Beneath a tree whose branches
are tight and yellow as a rose
-bud, the dead are only half
buried. Skin paper thin,
bones glowing, they stir
as if digging their own way
in or out of this unholy ground.

Last night we were a mountain,
unscaled. Our love was Himalayan.
We must have slept an epoch.
Overnight a glacier cut across
a continent and split us into

cliffs confronting one another:
two prehistoric creatures
about to battle for the same
empty village for our breakfast.

*   *   *

The Making of the Day

My wife is
cooking breakfast.
Bacon sizzles.

On the lawn
a bird thrashes
in the grass,

a young girl
under her
first man,

and I finish
a new poem.
The afternoon

is hot, the air
oppressive.
My fan whirrs.

My wife hums
to herself,
hair clinging

to her face,
the rusty hooks
of our days:

in her eyes
the wish for
water, wings.

When we sit
down to dinner,
flies have

gathered on
the bird's
fierce eye.

*   *   *

Against Spring

My nose starts to itch:
a jonquil full of pollen
with a bee buzzing in it,
worming up into my brain
and out into the sunlight.

I become myopic.
The forsythia bush
outside our window is
a constellation of suns.

Rising from their own
reflections, fountains
springing from the dark
cool caverns in the earth,
willows by the river, love,
are angels, wild angels
on the muddy riverbank,
wholly still and silent,
the palest green, waiting.

Today the wind. God,
what a wind weeding out
my hair, the soft brown
stalks of last year's
zinnias left to frost
and snow, and rooting
out dead limbs
of trees that crashed
around me and exploded

shrapnel of their pulp
against my legs and chest.

It's spring again.
The infected cornea of ice
has fallen from our windows,
and raw light lacerates
the nerves and muscles
of our rooms. You air out
a winter's worth of blankets.
My seed seeds the lawn.

And at the private center
of your eyes where I have
never been, delicate, white
and fragrant as a May flower,
a love begins to bloom, wild
in the woods of your loneliness,
and it is not for me. Oh,
love, I am afraid of spring.

*   *   *

Science

Love, I've spent nights down
in the cellar pouring
over letters from your
past and younger lovers,
a monk becoming
blind and impotent.
I've parsed their sentences
and made meticulous charts
of the geneo-
logy of my ignorance
for the smallest clue
to rediscover you.

Every night I've heard you
moan and toss above me,
some wild saint asleep
alone in our bed,
scratching at the black thighs
of the air, the woolen
backs of blankets, while I
itched to be torn open
like a goat or bread.
At dawn I have come back
upstairs, my eyes ringed
as a voyeur's, to crawl
back into bed, still dumb,
and curl up against you.

I've learned nothing in four
years. Each day I un-
learn more. You move about
the house quiet as

calculus, a foreign
language my tongue will
never master. Even
when I'm deep inside you,
probing for my own dark
center, you remain
an aboriginal
superstition. You are
impenetrable.

You fall asleep, dream
and whisper the names
of wiser men who
solved that riddle that
you harbor like some
undiscovered and essential
element or atom.

*   *   *

Testament

And now our bedroom's sealed,
the tomb of Pharaoh
stirring with huge spiders,

reincarnations of ourselves.
Your kiss devours me.
Our bed is an anthill.

With every cave and crevice
of our bodies full of honey,
trembling liquid gold, our

words, the teeth of memory,
begin their work. But our
bones are secret passage-

ways winding down to the center
of the earth where, leaping
up like lava, mysteries

are still unearthed, where love,
an offering left by the living
for the dead, can crystallize.

And there, love, among undiscovered kings, we will not die.

❋   ❋   ❋

Angelic Orders

Angelic Orders

For Michael Margolin

> *If I cried out*
> > *who would hear me*
> > > *up there among*
>
> *the angelic*
> > *orders?*
> > > *—Rilke*

I

I've been seeing angels recently.
Green ones, mostly.
They look like trees.

Some are domestic: fruit trees,
maples, elms and oaks. They run
after me. They whine when I ignore
them and walk by. They pelt me
with acorns, spit syrup at my head.
They throw tantrums and break birds.

Some are olive trees rooted
for centuries in the stony
landscape of my memory's holy land.
Others are ethereal:
willows rising by the river,
shimmering with ecstasy.

I don't know what to make of one
of them. It's in my bedroom
every night. A cyprus, it's
dark green, almost black.

It is tall, serene. Or it trembles,
gathering a storm above a field of red
and fierce, intolerable poppies.
It is glowing softly, moaning.
It is waiting   waiting

II

Clocks are angels, too:
their phosphorescent faces
glowing pale green through
the night, clucking minutes
one by one and filling up
my room with incandescent
feathers. And radiators,
as I've said before, are
angels. The refrigerator
is an angel: squat and square,
guarding meats and vegetables
and milk inside the steady
cold of its folded wings
where a light mysteriously burns.

The rocking chair's an Early
American angel. Sometimes,
in the middle of the night,
I wake up and hear it
creaking softly, creaking
like the wrath of God or
the noise among dry bones
waxing louder and louder.

Flags are captured angels.
Flags are captured archangels
tearing their wing tips
on the wind and clawing
for escape. And blankets,
sent from such heights as

lovers come from, are angels.
Asleep, I am thin and white, stirring.

But doors are solid, flat
angels. They are always
there, pure as triangles,
faceless and essential,
locking me out of rivers,
barring me from fields,
from houses and from mansions
I must enter   I must enter

III

But that is only half
of it. The fact is
I don't only see

angels. I am one.
When I'm alone
at night, I draw all

the drapes, and in
that total darkness
I become an angel.

I stand stark still
and naked. I don't
stir until I feel

a fierce, unearthly
stirring in the pool
of my belly, the seed

of a thousand saviors
gathering like
a galaxy. My bones

are flutes for the word
of God, and sunlight
streams in my arteries.

At last, I glow—
all white. I tremble.
My hair is the moon.

Wingless, unfeathered,
I am translucent.
I am fleshless. Pure.

I rise. I hover
above the city.
I visit virgins.

    *   *   *

Flute Making

Cleave it, then,
trim off the leafy end,
those tough and bitter greens.
Wash it off and boil it
till the meat is bleached.

Take that clean bone
to the trembling desert
of the highest rooftop
and set it out to dry.

Keep watch over it.
Sit cross-legged and serene
in your most perfect lotus
moving with the sun and moon.
Let no shadow dampen it.
Beware of birds.

Let the sun dry out
the marrow. Lift the bone
up to your lips, gently
suck the yellow powder,
and with your breath's
open hand scatter its dry seeds.

Let the bone dry still,
still more. Let it dry until
it glows, until your eyes
are burning jets of fever.

And when the sun
and moon are burning

in the same blue eye,
when seeds clatter
in your hip bone,
when your tongue
is bone, when the bone
is pure and dry,

then hone one end
until it's smooth
against your lips,
until your tongue
is comfortable on it.

Carve out the stops,
absolutely round.
Decorate it:
exquisite scrimshaw
from a perfect tusk.

Now play it.
Make music.
High, pure notes,
inhuman octaves.

Love, play
that fine flute
of my right arm.

❀   ❀   ❀

Diseased

then tear it out

saw off the limbs starting
with the bright and tender
rooted in the sun

let them tumble wings
torn from unearthly birds

the sun moaning in the leaves
leave that bright blue
wound the scar of sunlight

the beast crouching by
the trunk will die

and then the trunk slice
it huge slabs down
until your saw is burning

gravel rings and rings
of imperceptible secrets
the amulets of gods

decoded and all defenses
stripped the beast is
dying in the sun

leave the roots for those
who come hooded and armed
with syringes and serum
mysterious as faces

the gorgeous beast is dead

＊　　＊　　＊

Sailing from Byzantium

I don't think I'd care,
ever, to be some
mechanical bird

perched on a president's
desk or twittering
for a couple matrons

up in Scarsdale, drowsy
on a few too many
martinis. I don't

think I'd like to be
a slave, either, cooking
inside an ancient

brass bull, or a Jew
for anybody's guests.
I'd rather stay right here.

In a cold water flat
on the lower east
side, or a farmhouse

in Maine's up-country,
in a kitchen catching
its two minute sun,

with my wife, still half
asleep, leaning on
the sink, making me

breakfast, I'd rather be
that white shelled egg
in the copper pot,

chirping as it boils.

*   *   *

Today

1

This morning I could
have walked on the eyes
of daisies, my blood

was so bright, my head
a whole swarm of bees.
My bones were wired,

transparent as wings
of dragonflies. I
had to think of things

like pyramids and sphinx,
ebony pharaohs,
a granite crucifix—

such weighty and grave
matters to anchor
my ankles to pave-

ments and gravitate
my pelvic cavity,
ground my soaring weight.

2

Today I could have
suffered martyrdom
or capital punishment

for my faith or sins,
with an addict's thirst
breathed huge gulps of gas,

knelt in a lion's den
and stretched my arms wide
open, sung and waited

for his kiss burning
on my throat, his paw
tearing at my belly.

Oh, today I could have
faced a firing squad!
I could have been

Stephen, Maximilian,
Chessman. I would have
welcomed any wound

to rid me of that beast
trapped behind my ribs
and clawing to get out.

3

All day today I would
have lain on the gold
beard of ripened wheat.

Poised like a fakir,
Francis in his wild
ecstasy above

bright tips of thorns,
I would have slept there
at the fierce center

of the open field,
arms outstretched,
my feet floating

on the heaving wheat,
knees hoisted sails,
my bare hips flashing

mackerel in moonlight.
I would have waited
until he came, leapt

from the spinning sun,
fished me from the field,
sifted me from chaff,

and ground me, ground me.
I would have waited
for him to devour me.

*   *   *

Death and Transfiguration

This morning on my way to class
to teach my freshmen how to write
a research paper on the mass
media, just as I was walking under
the railroad bridge running over
Iowa Avenue and heading West
across the river, just as I got
halfway across and a refrigerator
car full of frozen meats and another
and another and another rode
the rails of my hair, just then

        a lion roared,
        the day turned
        technicolor, I
        grew stereophonic
        ears, my eyes'
        screen stretched,
        and from the far
        wall of my skull
        a Vista-Vision
        flashed across
        by brain: My God,
        I'm in a movie!

At first I wondered: Should I tell
them? Should I, after calling
roll, jump up and shout: My Dears,
I have a very special announcement:

        I have been made to see
        we're only film and light,

reflections. I tell you
our skins are bits of glass
on screens, our bones are
celluloid. Listen, our words
are nothing but a track
of sound. We don't exist.

Any minute now, any minute
someone who is watching
all of this will stand
up. Any minute now
we'll be inside his mouth,
our wild faces flashing
on his teeth, our voices
screaming in his eyes
until he closes them and
wipes us out with his
eyelids and his tongue.

Today, class, I am telling
you all there is to know.
I'm telling you what Paul
and Isaiah saw, but never
told, but never told.

But, you see, it wasn't all that bad
a flick, and I got all involved in it.
I lost track of time and what I was
being paid to do. Every girl was
Doris Day: smiling, singing, sexy,

nice; every girl Elizabeth Taylor:
purple eyes and pearly teeth. The men
were Tarzan: bare chested, primitive,
loin cloths bulging with enough seed
to populate heaven and earth —or cool
and suave as Cary Grant preserved on LSD.

Marcello Mastroianni,
that was me:
dark, deep, corrupt,
but suffering from
absurdity.

And so, no one ever knew that
just as I was on my way to class,
and just as I was walking under
the Rock Island Railroad Bridge,
we had all   E X P L O D E D
I N T O   S T A R S

❖   ❖   ❖

Bombardier

I am falling
inside my dead
mother I am

falling through light
years of dark

rapids chew roots
the bark of trees
shattering boulders
with serrated foam

ice flashing in
the summer moonlight

from the lair
of my father's ribs
on the desert's shore
my bones are born

   ❖   ❖   ❖

Paratrooper

I've stopped holding on
weeks ago I gave up
rescue ghost and gravel

my fingers are soldered
to rock each bone taken
root a hundred veins

of ore in an unfathom-
able mine I am growing
out of the face of this rock

generals sailors
even presidents know
the grace of the earth eating

skull I am praying wild
birds to sacrifice my wrists
my feet have begun their ascension

❋   ❋   ❋

Fish

The morning liquefies.
I take one step, spring up,
and I am swimming
above branches of coral.
I breathe water. Delicate
fish dart through my eyes.
Gold and black, they are
angels. Inside my skull,
nesting in my lungs,
they sing shrill, barbarous
arias, chorals of kyries
at some inhuman pitch.
They are shattering my bones.

Nothing, nothing weighs me
down, not even the drought
of darkness sweeping across
the States toward Asia.
Men flicker like matches.
Whole cities are burning.
The Mississippi's brown
with blood. Still I am rising
higher and higher. Angels
are winging me toward
planets pulsing like pearls,
toward space infested with sharks.

❀　❀　❀

In the Beginning

As if called by a voice
inhabiting the sun
crouching on a hilltop
and brooding over suburbs,
they come from behind
the grey, loose bark
of trees, beneath a stone;
they rise from the bone
and flesh of cattle
steaming in the fields
and alleys; they come
from the folds and seams
of our damp clothes, and
from the roots of our hair.
They come from nowhere.

This morning the space
outside our window
filled with a universe
of seeds. Tonight swarms
of newborn insects
gather into galaxies
trembling blue and green,
inheriting the air.

And worms are stirring
beneath our soles,
rising to be crowned
princes of the earth.

*   *   *

IN ADVENT

On His Unborn Child

To My Wife

Cleopatra in the guise
 of Theda Bara plastered
  on our bathroom wall

has immortal longings
 every night about three
  in the morning, and with thick

papery flutters, rustling
 wings on the angel of death,
  collapses in the bathtub.

The Corvair's exhaust pipe
 and muffler have succumbed
  to road salt and to rust,

fallen, and every morning
 as we roar to class,
  monoxcidal fumes ride

the rush of cold air
 from the heater, tempting
  us to sleep and dreams sturdier

than those we've awakened
 from to go to every day,
  every morning, every night.

And poor Jack, the rare
 late autumn days have knit
  his jaw into thick clumps

97

of orange skin wilting; rot
  blisters on his lower lip;
    a grey moss beards his chin.

A month ago he was our own
  St. Elmo's fire smiling
    two-toothed above the lawn,

as we sailed through another
  year of strangers in this old hulk.
    Tonight the dull fire of his mouth,

hissing as it burns
  the soft pulp of his head,
    might be the foolish glow

of gas above a marsh or graveyard.
  Jack should be in bed,
    his head hollowing a pillow.

Jack looks like my grandmother,
  her face caving in to gangrene
    eating away inside her head

until she died, mouth
  open, an enormous foul hole
    behind her lipless grin.

And me, love, Christ, look.
  My pores are swollen: beads
    of skin cluster on my chin.

They tell me as I get older
   I look more like my grandmother
      when I smile. Last night I dreamed

she was sleeping beside you.
   She wore Jack's hollow head.
      Love, I dreamt I was dead.

Look, love, while you bloom,
   the rest of us decay.
      Flies buzz around our eyes.

But I'll have the muffler fixed.
   Tomorrow I'll dispose of poor Jack's head.
      Let the dying bury the dead.

And you, bloom to one
   inside you, one who'll live
      my grandmother's name,

my father's name and mine,
   a child born at Christmas time,
      my seed thriving in you, my slime.

❊   ❊   ❊

In Advent

For Basilike and Daphne

1

According to our calculations,
You were expected long ago.

But still you crouch inside
The cage of your mother's veins,

A creature conceived by another
Creature, winged, sacred, secret.

Others like you have been known
To be too early or too late.

And we've been always unprepared.
Advent is our only season.

2

Although this winter night's
Ablaze with shafts of lightning

Edged with mauve and echoes
With the roar of thunder

Like the sea crashing down
On a pursuing army,

What can I do? I can't
Deliver you from your captivity.

And once you've escaped
Into this wilderness

Where every night promises
No more than itself, and you

Have shown a measure of good
Will and a capacity to survive,

I'll be of no greater use
To you. I'm no one's delegate.

My laws are my own, shifting
With the sand I walk on.

I can't legislate for you, and
I won't promise you the land,

When I can't promise you today.
I'm amazed by every morning:

I sing and dance, even for the sand,
And praise the burning at my feet.

Baby, I'm a desert creature,
One of a nomad tribe, accustomed

To betrayal by the mirage of need.
But this is what I chose,

With David, Ruth and Paul: exile,
The terror of the constant sun

Obliterating every trace of prayer
And law from the ghetto of my tongue;

The wind demolishing my words,
Dust seeping in my bones;

Rats spying on my every wish,
Attacking every hope every night.

But this is what I chose,
Rather than complicity with prelates

Who, with a Nazi zeal,
Will execute their own,

Make candles of their fat,
Censers of their skulls,

Stoles of their embroidered skin—
Sacramentals for their rituals

To preserve the sweet, rich blood
Of their infected race.

I am obsessed by the memory
Of murdered friends.

In dreams I finger their bones
Like beads, burning.

Their ashes stir and glow
In the reliquaries of my eyes.

If you choose to search for
Still another atmosphere, Baby,

You'll have to find your own
Way out. I can't deliver you.

3

You'd think yours is going to be
Another virgin birth, redemption

In some Iowan farmer's stable,
Cornhusks for your cradle,

Attended by the Aga Khan,
Pope Paul and Martin Luther

King. I see them kneeling,
Wise in the wealth of silos,

Silent, round and solid
As the towers of old temples;

TV antennas, stainless steel
Angels on rooftops transmitting

Heavenly messages to farmhands
Dozing on the frozen hillsides.

4

Where do we go from here?
What frontier, sea or galaxy

Will we have to cross disguised
As night creatures, warming our hands

To the thin embers of twigs,
Feeding on cactus and raw fish,

Slaking our throats with salt
Water or juices of wild locust,

Like fugitives to find asylum?
What drunken governor, anxious

For the safety of his state,
Will sign your execution?

How many children will soldiers
Slaughter so you can live?

In what desert, jungle, city street,
Or campus will you wage the war

The rest of us keep losing
Every day? Each day conquered.

What friend will betray you
To the priests? What priest

Will sell you to the state?
Baby, we're all Black, all Jews.

Every minute is an exodus.
Hours roar like cattle trains.

Each day is an oven.
Our skulls wish for the bullet's kiss.

How many governors and good
Citizens will be saved by law and order?

Will I live because you died?

5

Baby, I don't know
If you've been fathered

To be a prince of peace
Or criminal. My name

In the official census
Is Joseph. All I can

Do is build a bed
And roof for you, supply

You with my name,
My blood and race,

My species; then, season
After season, wait.

   ❋   ❋   ❋

To Daphne on the Third and Fourth Days of Her Life

1

You live and breathe
in a simulated atmosphere,
rarified, behind a shield

of glass, protected
from our infected
air, your natural

habitat. I visit you,
a stranger to your needs,
touch and speak to you

with the help of media:
an intercom and nurse,
sterilized and masked,

disinfected intercessor.
Contaminated, dangerous,
I am still your father.

I'm your originator.
For centuries it seems
I watched you make

your way into my world.
With my ear pressed
against the wall of skin

that separated us,
I heard you swim from side
to side, primeval, precious

fish in my wife's sea.
I later felt the contours
of your spine, the probing

of your foot or fist, my
baby, still not quite
born, still not quite human

enough to breathe my air.

2

Today I bring you home.
I am prepared to sterilize
utensils, bottles, nipples,

boil the water you will drink.
If needs be, I'll sterilize
the sterilizer, eradicate

a whole race of bacteria
with a Hitler hysteria.
I'll be antiseptic.

But I can't purify
this air you'll breathe.
The air, the air—it is

diseased. It germinates
despair. It can't be
filtered of the shrieks

of burning tongues, throats
melting in Hiroshima,
Auschwitz or in Viet Nam.

Each day and night smells
of dead burnt fat and hair.
Each breath will grease

your lungs, atomic soot
will plug your throat.
What artificial respiration

can I provide for you?
Poems are my iron lungs.
These weird contraptions

pump and pump my chest,
pressure me to survive
each day. I live in

their chambers and praise
the current that makes
them work. But I

can't make a poem
strong enough to help
us both. No poet can

or will. Someday you
may discover or invent
your own machinery

to survive. Until then
we're still divided
by that wall that separates

the living from the dead.

❖   ❖   ❖

The Gleaner

For whatever we lose(like a you or a me)
it's always ourselves we find in the sea

—e. e. cummings

All day they've ringed and ringed
the wet enamel of my skull. I thought
a walk along the beach would rinse
away the memories of years and years
today. But the beach is littered with
its own debris: cracked shells rattle
over stones, like bones. And bones:
a rib bleached marrowless, smooth
and brittle as Eve's spine;
a leg burnt into charcoal, gnawed;
the pale pink shells of last year's
picnickers. Under my feet dry
kelp, an ancient foetus, fractures.

What am I looking for in the litter
of strangers and storms? Pearls
iridescent as eyes? The key of
a sunken treasure chest tumbling out
beyond the reef? Fossils of fallen
angels, petrified proof all doesn't
start and won't end here? My blood
is already white with salt. My bones
are shivering for the kiss of some
wild lover in the night. My father's
fingers have begun to turn to snow
and mine are rooting in the sand.

I look down into small pools, poems
that are forming, in defiance,
between rocks: sea grasses bloom green,
gold and delicate. And mussel shells:
soft and cool and firm and white

as the inside of my lover's thigh
curved beneath the moon. She lay
on her side discovering my face
the way I touch, explore this shell,
her finger tracing some old mystery
our days together solved forever.

In the sand the imprints of birds
are the hands of murdered friends
clawing for revenge; the backs
of crabs are red and torn, mouths
of forgotten lovers without tongues;
anonymous organs shrivel in the sun
—not a shard of evidence that
any one of them forgave me as he fell.

Darkness is a gentle hand come to toss
the sun across the belly of the bay.
Gulls hover over me, their eyes
as sharp and yellow as their beaks.
They're waiting for my shell
to crack so they can come, swoop
down in their own ecstasy and greed,
clean out my skull and leave it
to the sun and sea, relentless tides.

We are the last inhabitants of this
planet. Each day the sun dissolves
one more degree. Only scavengers survive.
And soon that heaving sea, blood,
birds and every other scrap of memory
will end, disintegrate, a dust storm
storming that last cold space beyond
all forgiveness, love and history.

❋　❋　❋

Script Prospectus

To His Wife

I'm scared out of my mind,
scared to death. Looney
tunes run on inside my head,

scores for mad scenarios.
Any day now I'll be waiting
for a subway and someone

gone berserk on smog will
shove me: neck and ankles
sizzling sparks, a train

will dismember me. Any day
on my way to talk to my
conscientious class on

the ways and means of poetry,
another Whitman boy, obsessed
by his belief in words, will seize

me in his sight and, balanced
on a ledge or trembling
by a window, will blast my head

wide open. Darling, any day
now I'll make love to you
and in the thrashing of your

frenzy you'll slip a knife
into my spine, or I'll come
home and toss our baby into

our roaring hearth. I'll drink
from a bubbler chilled
by a live wire meant for that

girl behind me and immolate
myself by accident, with cal-
culated satisfaction jab

a jugular while shaving, lose
my shirt at craps, or step
into an open elevator shaft.

Darling, I'm not paranoid.
But as if invisible agents
of some unsuspected enemy

emptied vials of secret
formula into our reservoirs,
sprayed our orchards while

we slept, these days even
the most gentle of our friends
and citizens blink, shiver,

and are monsters, products
and victims of a supreme
mad scientist. Young men mix

a pig's blood with their own
and pour it into filing
cabinets. Others make huge

bonfires of their bones and hair.
A mother carves the heart out
of her four year old son's chest

and makes a sacred menorah
of his ribs. A couple
vaccinate their children

with insecticide to collect
double indemnity. And, Lord,
these aren't even metaphors

or scripts for class B flicks.
But the daily news. Something's
wrong. I must write my congress-

man, demand a national enquiry.
The only sanctuary left is
exile or asylum. And hell, no,

darling, I won't go. Still
until this mystery is solved,
until we've discovered what

inhuman agent is responsible
for all of this, every time
I hear someone running hard

behind me or laughing loud
and invisible, I'll be scared.
And every night inside my head

the same old horror show: any
day some stranger, relative or
friend will kill me. Or you will.

   ❂   ❂   ❂

Sunday Morning

I've tasted blood all week—
a few bad teeth, trench mouth,
who knows, cancer of the jaw
corroding the roof and bars
of my tongue's cage hanging
in the Northeast corner
of the Great American Kitchen.

I sit in Miss Washington's
Diner in New Britain, Conn.,
eating a number five breakfast
and reading the news of the week
in review in the Sunday *Times:*
the Pope has prayed for peace
again in St. Peter's Basilica;

in Saigon two monks sang
their final hymn, incense
ascending toward the sun
like Abel's latest offering;
and another hero has intoned
an epiphany on his men.
The last mass is over now,

the hour's fattened lamb slain
and eaten, and the faithful,
hungrier than ever, hurry
home to soup and sandwiches,
the comic strips and news
of how a hero, monk and Pope
waged war with prayer this week.

My coffee's laced with blood;
blood on each mouthful of eggs.
I haven't been to mass.
I may be victim of a cancer.
Still I sit here in this diner,
dying, damned and chattering
about the liturgy of others.

❋   ❋   ❋

Famine: 1966

To: Lyndon Baines Johnson
For Philip Berrigan

Sir, the grass is withering.
Trees are bare baskets
in a famine. Bloated shadows
of cattle balance on the dull
edge of the moonlight's horizon.
This November night is deadly
still, the air contaminated,
sweet with the hot, fierce breath
of leaves —a plague spread
on our lawns. Our neighbors
sleep, stricken with disease.
Young men die out of season.

   ❋   ❋   ❋

Famine: 1970

To: Richard Milhous Nixon
For Daniel Berrigan

The cry of frogs rings the island, rings,
bullets ricocheting off raw steel. Spring.
Tonight the full moon rises pure, precise,
and deadly cold. Everything will freeze.

Trees petrify, their first and fragile
leaves the clatter of slate chips. In
the garden sharp white shoots are glowing
bones of young men rising in revenge.

Buds on bushes fall and shatter, empty
eggs and skulls of a generation turned
to salt. Our eyes turn and, marble, shine.
Our hands and feet root into veins of lead.

Our mouths already fill with sand.
And beyond the moonlight, in the dark dawn
will never break, we can hear the long and
eager moan of boulders as they mate and spawn.

❋   ❋   ❋

Hands March 14 1968

For Ruth Rosenau

the sun is dying in my hands

this buzzing drills my bone's enamel
and spreads its swelling poison

darkness in my palms chains
planets blinking in captivity
furious orbits their riot

burns the wiring in the walls and
without a word the gates swing open

to the fine fire of feathers
thrashing in my hands its pulse
more rapid than my own

if I wanted to I'd crush
this sun today I'm born
again I let it fly
free away from me

into the sky into the dark
of a church my mother
the land and domes of capitols
into eternity

I will be cold with nothing
to do my hands unattended

links dissolving in the wind nets
overrun with larvae big as fish
the rust of these screens
whistles in the dark

all about me my hands
ring in the grass jars shattered
by bullets pieces growing dark
they'll never be filled again

I renounce all contents and possessions

unlocking prisons I loosen
havoc on the city bodies
float in the canals rats are
ravenous for the eye of women
and fire leaps from rooftops
desperate angels and armies
in wild anabasis   that is that
last gesture of tyrants

❋   ❋   ❋

The Dream

For David DeTurk

> *Dazzling and tremendous, how quick the sun-rise would kill me,*
> *If I could not always send sun-rise out of me.*
>
> *—Walt Whitman*

> *The world catches fire.*
> *I put an unbearable light*
> *Into breath skinned alive of its garments. . . .*
>
> *—James Dickey*

> *I have risen to a body*
> *Not yet born,*
> *Existing like a light around the body,*
> *Through which the body moves like a sliding moon.*
>
> *—Robert Bly*

We are infested with light.
It gathers on the floor of the sea
that tides in the cave of our pelvis;
it sprouts on the limbs of our lungs,
branches over cliffs in our brain,
a bush burning law in a nation.

An organism from an alien world
rocketed down to test and possess
the planet, it feeds on the darkness
that breeds in the core of our cells,
on the pure filtered air in our blood.
Overnight millions of filaments

root and are thriving. By morning
our skin is transparent, our bones
are black, and we're radioactive,
barbarously bright. Ablaze
with amazement, we stay in our
bed all day, eclipsing the sun

in its orbit. Afraid we'll diffuse,
we don't move, not a muscle
or bone or an eye-beam. Still
by noon we can feel citizens
disintegrating on streets,
murdered by light. Seasons

accelerate. In the wink of an eye
blossoms are apples that ripen
flames, and clusters of grapes
are coals. Buffalos burn to a crisp
on the spit of their bones. The sea pulls

to a dead stop. Whales rise like zeppelins.
By midnight the earth is pure mineral
ore, melting to white at its center.
Ravenous, we embark

❋   ❋   ❋

The Coming

For Michael Waters

They're coming. Every night
I hear them coming: the whine
of their ships' incredible

annunciations far above
the cornfields at the city's
edge in the enormous dark,

among the stars. Only dogs
and others like me hear them.
Their fantastic engines ring

grace in our bones. One day
they won't simply hover over
fields, visions for a few in-

somniacs. But they'll land.
They'll land swiftly, without
warning, right in the centers

of cities. As if promised
for centuries, they will dis-
embark, radiant, inhuman and

glorious as gods stalking virgins.

*   *   *

Totem

For Sandi and Tony Piccione

Year in, year out I've shed my skin
and hair, my teeth and sperm,
perfect invisible antlers. Animal,
I've moulted names and friends.

Bones of strangers blow like bugles.
Hands ring. Tongues roll. A mob
of admiration starts to break and crush.

My ghosts roam the streets and wail.
I am arriving to myself.

   *   *   *

Easter Sunday

For Hanny and Bill Heyen

All moisture's been sucked out of me.
I've turned in and on myself. Layers
of stale pastry, my skin flakes: Buddha
crumbling at last and falling into place.

In the basket of my dust, my friends
will find what was twisted in me,
always grating on my ribs: a thin
and indestructible scroll, undecipher-

able ancient characters I could never
understand: *You will live forever.*

* * *

The Author

A. Poulin, Jr., was born in Lisbon, Maine, in 1938. He received a B.A. from Saint Francis College (Biddeford, Maine), an M.A. from Loyola University (Chicago), and an M.F.A. from the University of Iowa. He has taught at the University of New Hampshire, the University of Maryland in Europe and at Saint Francis College where he was Chairman of the Division of the Humanities. He is currently teaching at the State University of New York at Brockport. He and his wife, Basilike, have one daughter, Daphne.